Contents

Along the riverbank

Where are we?
We are by the river!

The water ripples and the sunlight sparkles.

5

Reeds and rushes

Reeds sway in the breeze.

Bulrushes have thick, fluffy, velvety heads.

7

Dragonflies

What an amazing insect!

Its wings are see-through.

Trees and flowers

Trees bend over the water.

Colourful
flowers grow.

11

Frogs

A frog sits in the water.

Those legs are great
for jumping.
Hop hop!

13

Under the water

Minnows look like little arrows in the water.

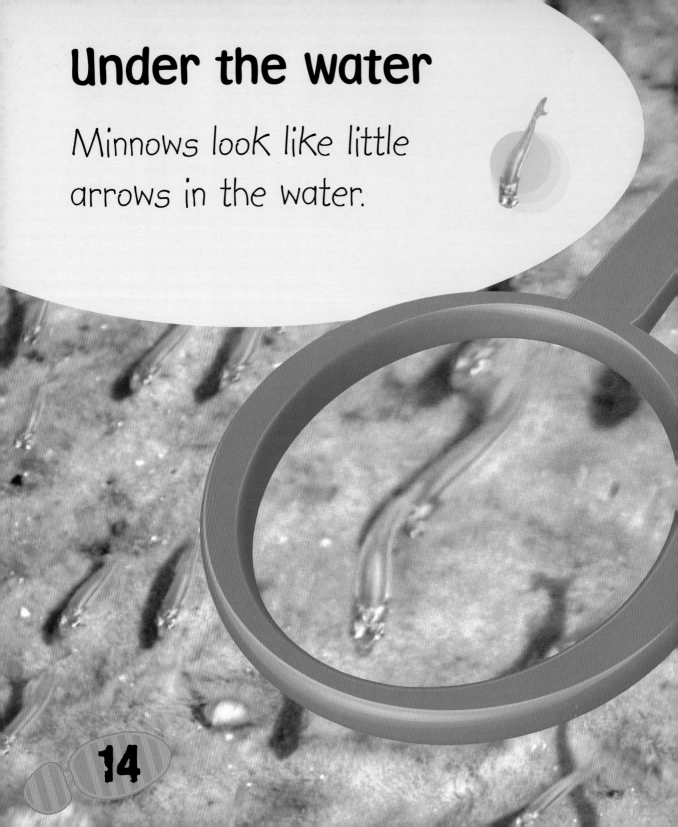

Bigger fish swim in the river too.

15

Fishing for food

This heron is fishing.

Dinner time!
He's caught a fish.

17

Riverbank families

Goslings look like little balls of fluff.

They are great
swimmers though!

19

Playtime

Otters have fun in the water.

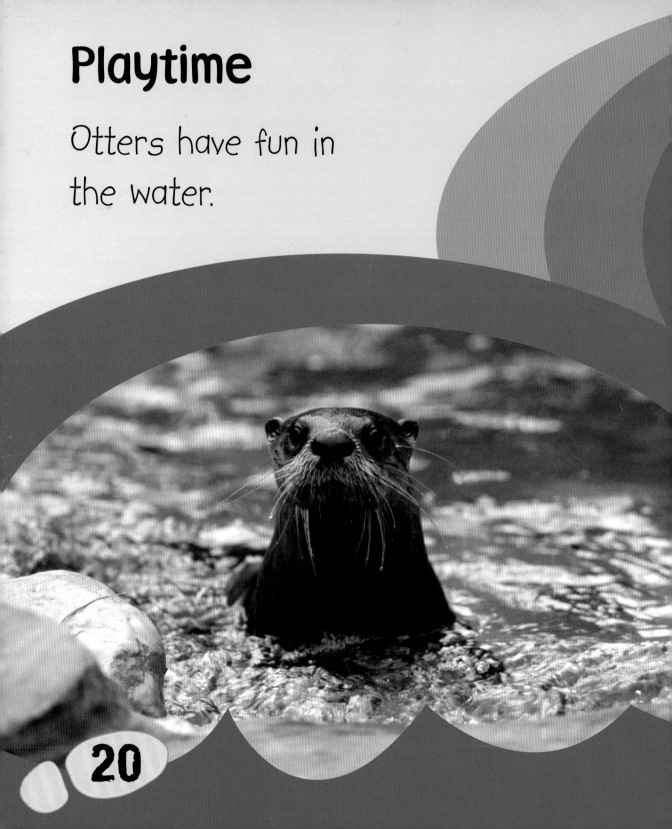

They play together.
Splish splash!

Goodbye river

Someone has come for a bedtime drink.

Take one last look.
Time to go home.

23

Index

Notes for adults

This series encourages children to explore their environment to gain knowledge and understanding of the things they can see, smell, hear, taste, and feel. The following Early Learning Goals are relevant to the series:

- use the senses to explore and learn about the world around them
- investigate objects and materials by using all of their senses as appropriate
- find out about living things, objects and events they observe
- observe and identify features in the place they live and the natural world
- find out about their environment, and talk about those features they like and dislike.

The following additional information may be of interest

Exploring the natural world at an early age can help promote awareness of the environment and general understanding of life processes. Discussing the seasons with children can be a good way of helping them understand the concepts of time, patterns and change. Identifying features that people share with insects and animals can promote understanding of similarities.

Follow-up activities

- Encourage children to think and talk about why people should take care of the environment and not damage plants or harm animals.
- Ask children to describe the sounds they might hear by a river.
- Use the animals featured in the book to get children moving. Ask them to show you how fish, frogs and dragonflies move.

24